# Fibredancing

## Book One: Brooches, Bracelets, Rings & Things

Original Textile Jewellery Designs
Using Free-machine Embroidery
By Carol Coleman

Fibredancing: Book 1 Brooches, Bracelets, Rings & Things

Copyright © Carol Coleman, 2007

Photography by Carol Coleman

SBN 10: 0-9551677-9-5

ISBN 13: 978-0-9551677-9-9

Published in 2007 by Word4Word

8 King Charles Court, Evesham, Worcestershire

www.w4wdp.com

Printed in the UK by Cromwell Press.

# Introduction

The projects, samples and finished jewellery featured in this book are all a combination of machine embroidery, hand embroidery and hand finishing with a decorative and useful end result. The fast start that you can enjoy with the help of your machine is complemented by the satisfying tactile experience of handwork that is so important to the embroiderer. I use cold water dissolving film extensively and I hope that for those of you who have not used it before, its discovery will lead you onto more adventurous projects and applications.

*A selection of colourful watch-straps, all made by Pauline Twyman.*

These pieces of jewellery are incredibly light and comfortable to wear and have become my first choice when travelling. Their value is slight compared to more traditional forms of adornment, so you need not take your valuables away with you. These pieces can be crammed into a suitcase or handbag yet still look good when you put them on.

My textile jewellery has proven to be surprisingly hard wearing and durable and can be washed when necessary too. You can make jewellery in many different designs to cover all eventualities. Even cheap watches can be made to look special with a designer strap providing an attractive accessory; you can have one in every colour for all occasions. I have tried to include a variety of styles and items with a wide appeal for all ages and tastes for anyone to produce their own art to wear.

# Materials & Equipment

## Embroidery foot

I always advise the use of an embroidery or darning foot, which together with the lowering of the feed teeth allow the free movement of the fabric, but hold it down sufficiently to reduce the occurrence of skipped stitches. The foot also reduces the risk of piercing your fingers. They come in a variety of shapes and sizes and materials. I have one embroidery foot and one darning foot. The embroidery foot holds down the fabric well and is an open C shape that lets me see what I am doing, but the open arms of the C sometimes get hooked up on loose fibres or threads. The darning foot is a larger closed D shape and works well on fat layers and fluffy surfaces. The make and model of your machine will dictate which feet work best for you.

## Sewing machine

Your sewing machine is the first vital ingredient to a successful stitched piece. You do not need an expensive one that has a multitude of functions; everything in this book has been created on a basic sewing machine using only two stitches, a zigzag and a straight stitch. You may need to make small adjustments to the bottom bobbin tension, as metallic or other threads are used for the bottom thread and can be as visible as the top thread.

Your machine must be under your full control, so one that runs away with you and does not allow careful stitch by stitch progress at moderate speed will only lead to severe frustration and a very disappointing result. Check your machine handbook for advice under free-machine embroidery or darning, where you should have instructions on how to prepare your particular make and model. My machine is a Bernina 1000, the most basic one they made when I bought it.

Do not drink alcohol when operating your machine. The advice for some medicine about not operating machinery while taking it applies to sewing machines too, particularly in free-machine mode!

*Embroidery foot*   *Darning foot*

## Needles

Your choice of needle is just as important as the machine itself. No matter how good your machine is, or how smooth its operator, if you are not using the correct needle for your project then you will have difficulties with fraying and breaking threads. Where we usually match needle type and size to the fabric we are using, in the case of machine embroidery, the needle should be matched to the thread. I have found that three types of needles accommodate most of the threads you are likely to use; Embroidery, Metallic and Topstitch in size 14. I find the slightly 'frosty' textured threads, such as Madeira's Supertwist, need a Topstitch size 16 for the best results. If you are new to machine embroidery, practice with your chosen fabric, threads and needle before beginning a project.

## Hoops

I prefer to use an ordinary wooden hand-embroidery hoop when free-machining, working inside the well, with the inner hoop pushed through slightly proud of the outer one to ensure good contact with the machine surface. Some machines do not allow much space to put these hoops under the foot, so you must work with what you can.

I often work by eye and in order to orient myself and not lose my place, I always have the screw for the hoop denoting the top of the work, with the end facing right, as I am right-handed. This lets me adjust the hoop or film if necessary without taking it off the machine or cutting any threads. I use a hoop big enough for the project, but no larger than necessary, as the larger the hoop the more slack is likely to get into the film. There are various sizes of square hoops with rounded corners available now that are ideal when making long strips such as bracelets, allowing you to manoeuvre a large hoop more easily on your machine. I have also seen a triangular one!

## Cold water dissolving film

There are numerous films available to us now, my advice is to try them all and see what suits you best. I work with three that seem to cover most of my needs: the thicker film Romeo for big projects that are unsuitable to put in an embroidery hoop; Vilene Solufleece, or Solusheet, (an opaque material) for when I am demonstrating, hand sewing, or need to follow a precise, drawn design; and any thin variety for day-to-day usage - using it double for humid conditions.

I haven't found a single film that provides all the qualities for every project, but there are enough choices to accommodate different needs and requirements. Keep your dissolving film securely in an airtight container and out of direct sunlight as it will become brittle with age and will dry out and become difficult to use very quickly if you don't store it appropriately.

Equally, if you allow it to become wet or significantly damp, it will stick together or partially dissolve and be almost useless. All the smallest scraps of film can be saved up and recycled by dissolving them in a jug of water, pouring the fluid into a perfectly flat tray and allowing it to evaporate. This usually takes a couple of days, but when all the moisture has gone the film can be peeled off the tray (scrape the edge with a spoon if you have trouble lifting the first bit) and you will have a usable piece of film made to any thickness from the tiny waste scraps.

## Thread

I always recommend the use of quality, recognised, branded threads as they are more likely to be consistent in colour, strength and colourfastness. Using the best quality ingredients will give the best results. Always buy enough thread for a project as dye lots can vary considerably and manufacturers can discontinue products at any time. The required quantities of fabric are small, but comparatively large amounts of thread are needed for all the fringes, edges and embellishments and are difficult to estimate. Look for metallic threads that are not too scratchy to wear next to the skin and that will work smoothly in your machine. Try out lots of different products and brands to understand how they look and behave.

*Metallic thread*

## Dissolving thread

I use this thread extensively as tacking, as it just rinses away with the dissolving film and I do not have to think about the boring process of removing tacking stitches. It is often available in patchwork and quilting supply shops. Using a matching machine embroidery thread as a tacking is an alternative if you are likely to forget to remove tacking stitches.

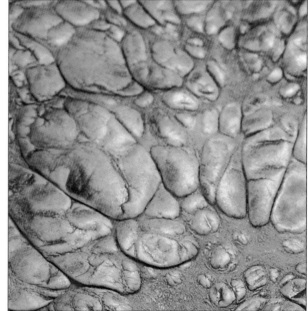

05

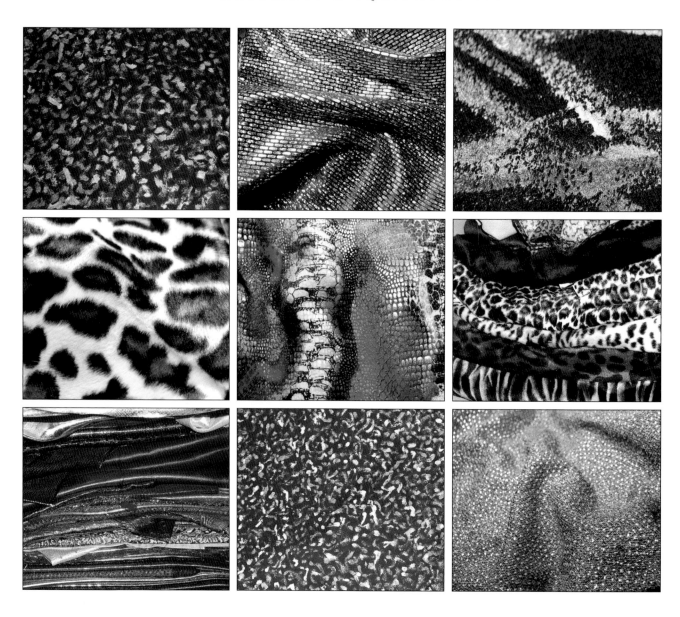

## Fabrics

I use a wide range of fabrics in my work. I now look at everything in all departments, as it is surprising which fabrics make good jewellery. Plain fabrics can be startlingly used by adding outrageous embellishments, and 'in your face' holographic or metallic fabric can be very good when used for small pieces.

One of my best discoveries was some good quality black woollen fabric, the closely woven, brushed sort that makes fine quality blazers. I used metallic fabric paint in small random splotches on the surface; the paint looked luminous and the background an even more intense black. I used three colours and changed one colour for a different one every few inches. This ensured that I had a large piece of useable fabric that gradually blended from one colour range to another without any sudden changes, so it helped to reduce waste.

I don't use silk very often as it frays so easily, isn't very hard wearing and can stain if you leave any dissolving film residue in the fabric.

Look out for fine, knitted fabrics that have a bonded or printed surface as they do not fray like a woven material and are easier to manage. The brown fabric shown in the bracelet sample on page 17 is a wonderful furnishing fabric that looks so much like leather that it fools everyone. It is important to feel the fabric before you buy, as it must be touchable if it is to be comfortable to wear.

## Foam

The inclusion of foam provides body and resilience to the
jewellery; without it, permanent creases and curling will occur
in time and make the pieces look tired and old. I use Softsculpt,
Plastazote or Funky Foam and they have given good results
and proven long lasting.

*Softsculpt*

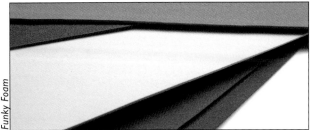

*Funky Foam*

## Recycling

I firmly believe in re-using and recycling old things. Look at
your old junk jewellery that you haven't worn in years and see
what elements of it could be snipped with a pair of pliers to
provide a completely new bit of decoration. Broken jewellery
is just begging to have a new life.

If you lose an earring, save the other one to incorporate into
a new piece of original textile adornment, and before you get
rid of your old clothes look carefully at the fabric to see if it
has further potential as a piece of textile jewellery; soft well-
washed fabric works very well as a backing or lining.

Look out for Tyvek envelopes; one large one goes a long way.
They are easily recognised as they have a waxy feel and you
can see the compressed fibres if you hold them up to the
light. Tyvek is difficult to tear, but easy to cut with scissors or
pierce with a needle and takes acrylic paint beautifully. Cut off
the glued edges and discard, as they are useless for
incorporating into the jewellery.

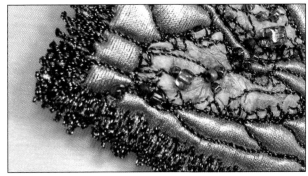

07

# Preparing For A Project

### Preparing for a project

Prepare your sewing machine for free-machining by lowering or covering the feed teeth, adjusting the tension if necessary and attaching an appropriate embroidery or darning foot according to your machine manual. When you have chosen what kind of thread you want to use, put in a machine needle that is appropriate for that thread.

All of these projects involve the use of cold water dissolving film, so you need to ensure that all materials used are colourfast and able to go through a hand wash. Any fabrics you have painted yourself should be heat set where required before you begin, as you may be including heat-sensitive materials such as Tyvek or Softsculpt. When painting Tyvek or other heat-sensitive material, use an acrylic paint as it is permanent when dry and does not require heat setting.

When putting dissolving film or material into a hoop I have found the following way of doing it gives the tautest result, without tearing or damaging the film.

With clean, dry hands at all times:
Check that the inner ring will go easily into the outer one, but is not so slack that it falls through.
Place the outer ring on a flat surface, screw at the top with the head facing right if you are right handed.  Drape the film over the top, allowing a couple of inches beyond.
Place the inner ring over that and gently push it inside.  If it is difficult, relax the screw a little and try again.
Pick up the hoop and working all the way around gently pull the film tight.  Tighten the screw a little and work around the film once more.  Continue to work the film and screw tighter until you can do it no more.

Pushing the inner ring through until it is slightly proud of the outer one will give good contact with the machine and help to eliminate the occurrence of skipped stitches and frayed and tangled threads.
To get the best results from these projects, you do need at least a little experience of free-machine embroidery. If you have not done any for a while, a warm-up session on some scrap fabric is advisable. Try drawing shapes with your needle, geometric, simple animals, flowers, etc. and try writing your name.  Practise stitching over holes in the fabric too and also reversing over lines of stitching you have already done. All these exercises will give you confidence and help you develop a smooth operating speed and even stitches.

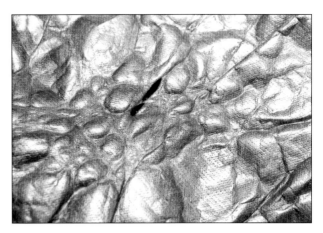

*Painted and heat-distressed Tyvek*

*Warm up by drawing shapes with your needle*

09

# Brooches

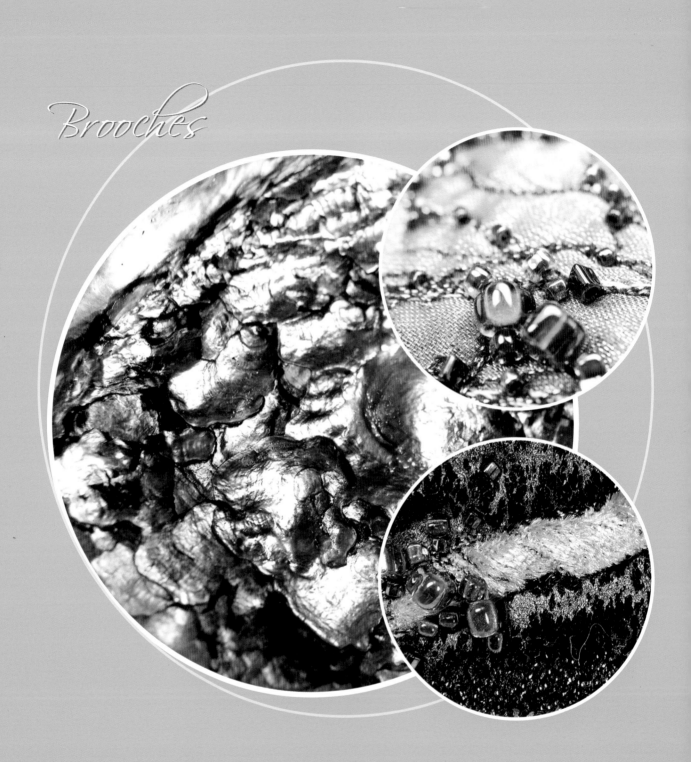

I have put these types of jewellery together in this book because of the way they are constructed. Each is a simple sandwich comprising a top decorated surface, a middle layer of foam to provide body and resilience and a base layer chosen for its colour and texture to finish the piece appropriately. I advise the use of fabric that resists fraying, as such small pieces can disintegrate quickly if you use a fragile, loosely woven fabric. There are some interesting finely knitted fabrics, unusual furnishing fabrics, and some lovely silky fake fur in the shops. The Christmas season is a good time to look for flashy exotic material and always check out the fabrics aimed at theatres and dance studios. You only need very small pieces - you might have just what you need from the leftovers of another project. The top surface can be built up with snippets of bright fabric on a dark background, or shiny on matt, metallic with fur or velvet, and in any colour. The combinations are limited only by your imagination or supplies, but always check for colourfastness before you begin. Beads, embellishments and hand embroidery are applied at the last stage.

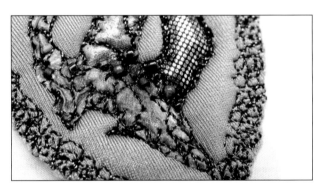

**Brooches**

Requirements

Foam - Softsculpt, Plastazote or Funky Foam
Fabric - small pieces of fabric and tiny bits of non-fraying embellishments such as Tyvek, Angelina, fake fur, painted Vilene etc.
Threads - machine embroidery threads to match or complement your choice of fabric
Machine needles suitable for the threads you have chosen
Beads
Small embroidery hoop
Cold water soluble film of your choice
Brooch pin
Beading thread and beading needle

Brooches are the easiest to start with because they can be any shape, do not need to be made to fit, are subject to less wear and tear and are not worn next to the skin. You can make just one simple design or produce several shapes independently and then put them together into a more complex arrangement that gives more depth or movement.

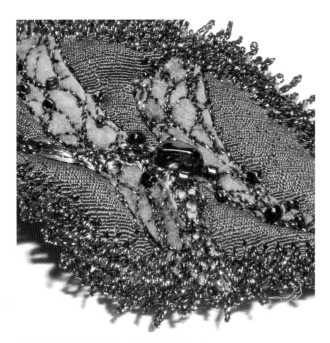

*A leaf shape with whiskery straight stitch edge*

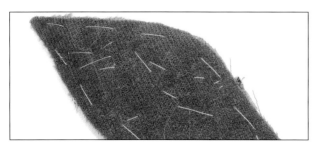

*Brooch back*

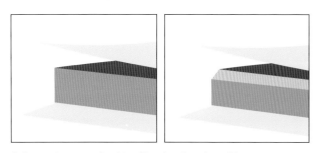

*Before tacking onto dissolving film, chamfer edges of foam*

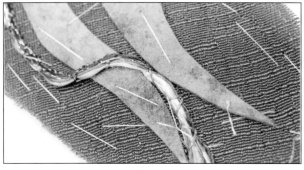

*Embellished sandwich ready to stitch*

**A leaf shape with a whiskery, straight stitch edge**

Materials: Plain green fabric with two pieces of painted Vilene and a small piece of cord to decorate. The base is a plain dark green brushed fabric.
Thread: Madeira FS2/2 Colour No 424, pale gold on top and 490, variegated green as bottom thread. Both the top and bottom threads are seen, so consider the choice of bottom thread as carefully as the top.

Cut a template out of paper or thin card exactly the size and shape for the brooch that you wish to make. Use it to cut out a piece of foam that is two or three millimetres thick, by placing the template on the foam and drawing around it with a pen, or using a pencil to make an impression and then cutting with scissors or a craft knife.

Tack the top surface fabric you have chosen to the foam and trim it almost to the foam, leaving about 1mm of fabric beyond.

Tack the chosen base fabric on the other side of the foam and trim that to the foam as with the top. This method of assembly is the most accurate way to prepare the sandwich of three layers.

As you machine-stitch into it later, the foam squashes a bit and can squeeze out from between the layers like a soft sandwich filling, so trim it thinner now. With small sharp scissors, chamfer along both perimeter edges of the foam at an angle to reduce its thickness.

The top layer can now be embellished with scraps of fabric, painted Tyvek, painted Vilene, fur fabric, etc. – anything that is decorative, resists fraying and allows a needle through. The edge of the brooch for about $1/4$ inch (6 mm) will be completely covered with stitching, so make allowances for that when placing the decorative bits on the top surface. Tack each piece down firmly, as it will have a tendency to move once you start machining. Care and accuracy at this early stage will give the best results at the end.

Hoop up the dissolving film as tautly as possible into a hoop big enough to take your piece, its fringing and the spare space you need around the edges for the machine foot, and tack your brooch securely onto the film. Never stitch your piece to the loose film and then hoop it up as this is likely to distort your fabric. Always tack rather than pin as the layers need to be secure, and pins can also distort the whole thing.

Proceed to embroider with the machine by stitching a medium width sparse zigzag around the edges first, to firmly secure the brooch to the film, and then stitch down any surface additions with straight stitch. When you have done this, it is time to remove any tacking stitches if you have not used dissolving thread.

With your machine set to straight stitch, begin to make the whiskery edges by working around the edges of the brooch, moving the hoop smoothly. Stitch forward onto the film and back onto the fabric, progressing carefully along the edges until you reach the point that you started. Go around again, filling any gaps or sparse places as you move.

You need to bring your stitching well back onto the fabric or your decorative edging will part company with your brooch.

Continue to embroider (doodle) across the main body, in a design compatible to a leaf, adding further stitching to any applied pieces to cover any raw edges. Be generous with the stitching and make the thread an integral part of the whole design, not just an excuse to cover the edges, but don't flatten the entire surface with stitching as it will lose its three dimensional quality. As you progress with the machine stitching on the body of the brooch, you may notice that some earlier stitches appear loose. This is because the foam is becoming more compressed the more you stitch, so if you feel they need it, go over these loose stitches again to hold them down.

When you have decided that you have finished with machine stitching, cut out the brooch from the film (do not dissolve yet - the edging is best left encapsulated in the film until you have completely finished) and further embellish it to your satisfaction with beads, cords and hand embroidery to give it texture and dimension. Using a matching colour beading thread, stitch a brooch pin on the back, checking which way round you prefer to pin it, hiding your stitches within the existing machine stitches.

When everything is finished, rinse the brooch under the cold tap, gently rubbing and pressing it to get rid of the film residue. To dry - press gently with your fingers between layers of kitchen paper or an absorbent cotton towel to remove the bulk of the water and then leave to dry naturally on a flat absorbent surface. Alternatively, deliberately twist or shape the brooch into a more 3D shape and allow to dry in that position. When dry, wear it with pleasure.

*Secure by using a sparse zigzag round the edges*

*Make whiskery edges*

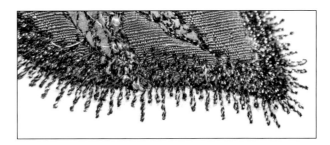

*Fill in any gaps*

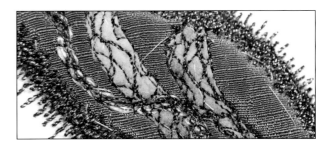

*Finished machining*

13

*Completed brooch*

*An oval brooch with satin stitch edging*

*Assembled sandwich, ready to stitch*

*Secured by zigzag and surface stitching complete*

*Second round of increasing zigzag*

*Machine stitching complete*

### An oval brooch with satin stitch edging

Materials: Top surface is black woollen fabric painted with metallic fabric paints and a small scrap of shiny gold and black fabric as a highlight, the base fabric is a dark pink brushed fabric.

Thread: Madeira FS2/2 colour no 426, a warm beige, for both top and bottom threads.

Begin as before, but after securing the edges onto the film with a sparse zigzag, complete all the stitching on the body of the brooch first.

When you have done that, go around the brooch edges with a slightly wider zigzag, wrapping the edge on the outside, and creep the stitches further onto the body of the brooch, but still just skimming the outside edge. Go around several more times, increasing the stitch width and filling in the gaps each time until you reach the widest setting on your machine. This method gives a smoother and flatter finish than trying to do it in one round. You can also do this edging by bringing back the feed teeth, setting your machine for ordinary sewing; just increase the stitch width with each zigzag round, and finish as before. Shapes such as a triangle with acute angles are more difficult to do with this finish as the corners are inclined to get bulky.

*Beaded and dissolved*

**A triangular brooch with randomly stitched edge**

Fabric: Knitted, patterned polyester in black, grey and orange.
Thread: Madeira Polyneon No 40 colour 1604, a soft
variegated green with peach, as both top and bottom threads.

This method is more suitable for fabric that is resistant to
fraying. Fur fabric or velvet give interesting effects with this
stitch as it can be flattened in some areas, giving a more
sculpted 3D appearance. Begin as before with a zigzag around
the edge.

The decorative stitching is just a meandering line that curls
and twists along the edge and just over onto the film. It is
best to go around two or three times to judge how thick and
how wide you want the border to be, and to keep the stitch
density even. You will also be able to judge when you have
done enough more easily by doing the stitching in this way.

These three methods of finishing the edges are the ones I
routinely use in the construction of my jewellery as they solve
the practical problem of sealing the raw edges while at the
same time look good. There are many other possible edgings,
but if the items are to be worn, then fancy or spiky finishes
may prove more nuisance than decorative.

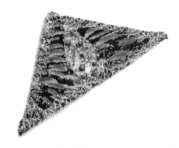

*A triangular brooch with randomly stitched edge*

*Assembled with small piece of painted Tyvek and ready to stitch*

*Zigzagged and Tyvek secured*

15

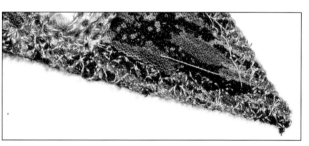

*Randomly stitched edge*

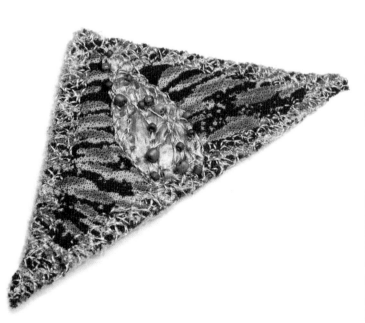

*Complete*

*Finished machining*

# Bracelets

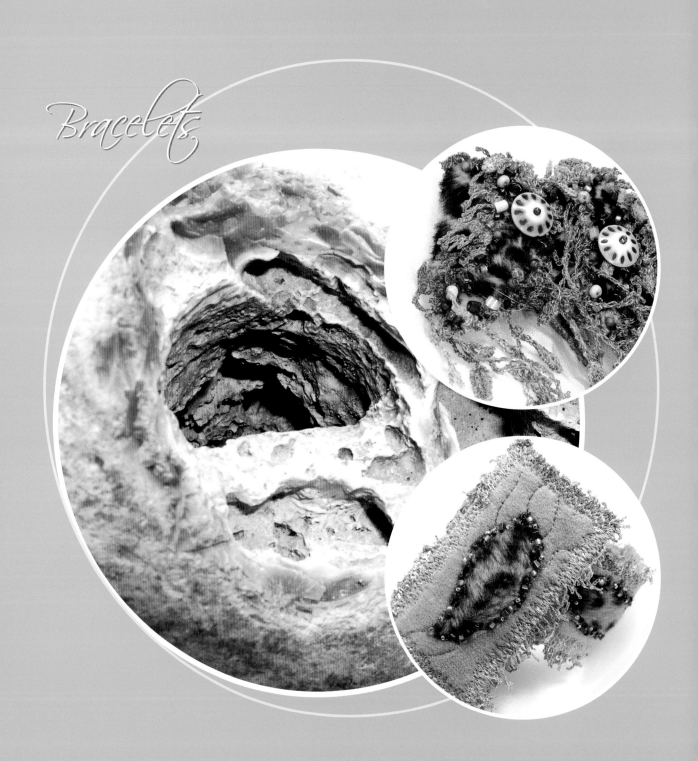

## Bracelets

Bracelets are an easy next step to try. They can be a simple
decorated band, constructed just like the brooches only a
different shape, or made up of separately made components
and assembled to make a more complex design. They are the
most likely items to suffer the hardest wear and tear, so avoid
fragile fabrics unless you plan a bracelet for special occasions
only.

Requirements

The same as for brooches except no brooch pin. You will
need larger pieces of fabric and foam, enough to go around
your wrist in one piece and also a small amount of Velcro in a
colour to complement your fabric.

These textile bracelets are made to fit like a watch strap, using
Velcro as a fastening and extra security added by stringing a
short stretch of beads as a safety chain. Made with three
layers of fabric like the brooches, but you need to consider
that the bottom layer will be next to your skin, so should be
soft and porous to allow moisture to move away from the
skin and not irritate.

First, make a template out of paper, remembering to allow
sufficient overlap around your wrist. The thicker the layers,
the longer the template needs to be; the dimensions will
usually fall between $7^1/_2$ inches (19 cm) and $8^1/_2$ inches (21.5
cm) for most female wrists and the sample shown is $1^1/_4$ inch
(32 mm) inches deep. Making additional elements separately
to add to the basic wristband is easy and you can achieve a
very complex-looking result without difficulty.

*A bracelet in two colours with a vintage button embellishment*

### A bracelet in two colours with a vintage button embellishment

Material: Woven imitation leather fabric.
Thread: Madeira FS 2/2 Number 482, variegated copper/gold
colours.
A single vintage button and some copper and gold coloured
beads provide the embellishment.

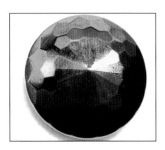

Using your template, proceed as for the brooch by cutting
out, tacking the three layers, mounting onto film and machine
stitching all the edges and over the body of the wristband. Do
some extra stitching over the full width for about an inch at
both ends in order to flatten these areas, as they are designed
to overlap under your wrist and it is best to reduce bulk
where possible. If you want a band that is made with only a
little stitching over the body, then you need to allow for its
bulk by adding extra on the length.

*Wristband sandwich*

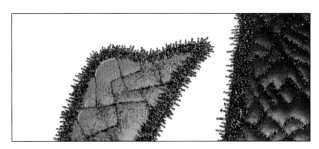

*Finished machine stitching*

17

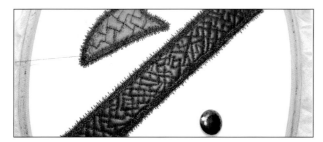

*Three elements of the bracelet*

Cut out a small piece of Velcro and securely stitch either the hook or loop side to one end of the bracelet as close as possible to the end. Turn over your piece and stitch the other bit of Velcro to the underside of the opposite end.

Cut out the band from the film and wrap it around your wrist to check the fit and placing of Velcro etc. Dissolve the bracelet and dry flat.

*Velcro at the end of the band*

Make the added top piece exactly the same as the brooches, embellish with beads etc. and arrange on the surface of the wristband, stitching securely using strong thread such as beading thread.

The safety chain is just a string of beads joining one end of the bracelet to the other. Always use beading thread and go through the beads at least twice. Check you can still pass the bracelet over your hand before securing permanently.

*Beaded and buttoned*

*Safety chain*

18

*Dissolved and ready to attach to wristband*

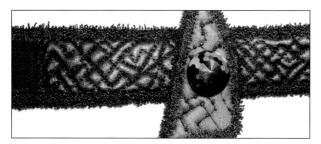

*Almost finished*

*Ready to wear!*

Longer fringes can be made by extending the stitching over the film and adding branches to the original strand. You must keep crossing the first line of stitches to keep locking on the branches so that they will be secure after dissolving.

Stitched shapes can easily be created on the ends of these strands by 'drawing' the shape you want in stitch and then creating a warp and weft across it by stitching all over it, first in one direction and then in the opposite direction. Make sure you include the original line of stitching within it so that it doesn't hang free in a loop after dissolving. By holding it up to the light, you will be able to see if you have missed any areas or any of the original line. These shapes can be beaded or embroidered further if you wish

*Longer fringes can be made with added branches*

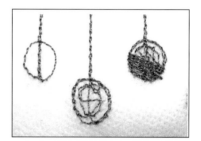

*Shapes made by creating a warp and weft with stitch*

*Beaded dangle*

*They can be any shape, but keep to the same construction method*

19

*Long beaded dangle*

# Watch Straps

## Watch straps

Requirements: as for bracelets.

Material: An old purple shot silk tie on the top and a recycled old dressing gown at the bottom.
Thread: Madeira FS 2/2 No 442, plain silver.
The watch is an old one bought from a charity shop

To begin with, these are made exactly like the bracelets. A plain wristband is made to fit your wrist with a Velcro fastening, it can be any width that you find comfortable and that suits your watch face.

Small looped straps of folded stitched fabric are created to attach the watch to the wristband; this has the added advantage of taking stress away from the watch fittings. Choose fabric fine enough to be folded over in three thicknesses yet will still fit through the gaps for the strap on each side of your watch.

Fold a strip of fabric over three times to fit the width of the aperture, with the raw edge just hidden underneath, and tack it in place. Secure it with the raw edge underneath to your ready-hooped dissolving film and stitch all over it, removing the tacking when secure. Cut it out of the film, measure a piece long enough doubled to attach to one side of the watch face and cut it to size. Fold it in half and reapply it to some more dissolving film. Stitch over the bottom third, leaving plenty of opening space at the folded end and cover the raw ends in stitching, creating a decorative shape with stitches on the film. When finished, do the other to match and dissolve both.

When dry, attach these small strips to your watch by removing the tiny pins on the sides of your watch, threading them through the folded ends of the fabric and securing them carefully back onto the watch.

It is now time to place these mini straps correctly onto the larger band. Never do this when it is placed flat, as when you try to wear it, the curve of your wrist will pull on the straps and the watch will be under too much tension. Put the large watchstrap on your wrist and mark where the mini strap ends should go, then remove and stitch them on by hand, further decorating the straps with beads or other embellishments. Finish with a safety chain of beads as with the bracelets.

You may have a watch with a different or more complex arrangement for the attachment. A little adaptation using braids, cords or ribbons to thread through more easily could be the answer. The raw ends can be finished off in the same way as fabric ones.

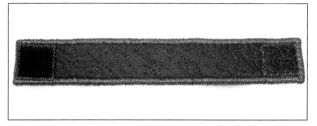

*Wristband prepared and worked with satin stitch edging*

*Fold over into three thicknesses and stitch decoratively all over*

*Fold and reapply to more dissolving film*

21

*Attach mini straps to watch*

*Attach watch to wristband*

*Earrings*

## Earrings

These earrings are just like miniature brooches, but you need to consider that both sides of the earrings will show, so the top and the bottom fabrics should both be attractive and decorative. Any size or shape can be made and also curled up loops will work.

It is quite easy to make completely reversible earrings by being careful and precise at each stage.

After machine stitching, bead the front and back simultaneously to avoid unsightly stitches showing, and attach an earring finding of a style and colour you prefer. You can sew them directly onto the findings, attach a tiny ring or even stitch a loop using machine stitching onto the dissolving film. They can be very large and dramatic earrings and yet remain very light to wear as long as you do not overload them with beads. Dissolve as for brooches.

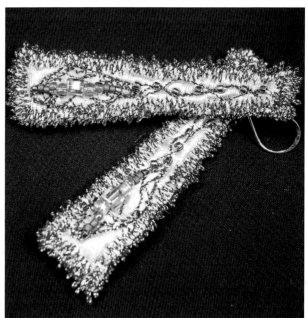

# Rings

## Rings

These rings encircle the finger and overlap decoratively on the top. They need a soft fabric as the layers will be next to your skin. You also need to consider bulk, so use finer fabrics. Choose the thread with care as some metallics will be too scratchy to wear with comfort.

Prepare by deciding how wide to make the ring and measuring the circumference of your finger, allowing a generous overlap for the top. This overlap can be made to different shapes and styles.

Start by making a template in paper or thin card and test it for size and shape. Make a sandwich of materials and continue exactly as for the brooches, but keep any fringing short. You could also make a decorative shape at the end with just stitch on the film. When the machine stitching is finished, cut the ring out of the film, dissolve and dry flat. Wrap the ring around your finger and secure the overlap with a stitch or two. Take it off and embellish with beads or gems of your choosing, then further secure the overlap, but leave part of it free to extend outwards. Alternatively you could make a loop of the extra fabric to make a raised top. You can make them as exotic and outrageous as you like.

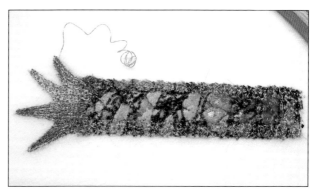

*Decorative shape stitched on the film*

*Multi coloured velour fabric ring with shaped stitched end. Real amber and beads*

*Overlap made into two loops with large tube bead in the centre*

*A long overlap cut to an elongated point and curled in a large loop on top. A stack of beads sewn inside*

# Artist Statement

*Carol Coleman,*

I am an evolved textile artist, with an evolutionary approach to design. I specialise in free-machine embroidered jewellery, boxes, art to wear and abstract wall pieces, often including fossils, shells, semi-precious stones and rocks and other textile techniques. By popular request, I have been teaching day schools in my speciality and giving illustrated talks on the development of my work to groups of embroiderers and other textile artists.

My work is inspired directly from the materials I use to create fantasy jewellery and wearable art, often recycling broken or found objects and giving them a new life in another form. As I discover new media and techniques, new ideas and inspirations follow and my work moves on to explore the potential of my latest discovery. Modern materials such as Tyvek, Plastazote, plastics and latex add to the versatility of traditional fabrics and thread. Part of my fascination with these things is the challenge of making attractive, durable and unique creations from unusual materials and unlikely sources. I also like the unconventional. I look to find new ways of wearing ornament, perhaps combining elements of conventional clothing or jewellery with the introduction of unexpected materials to make unique wearable art. The tactile quality of textiles combined with creating three-dimensional practical pieces is very satisfying.

Since 1999, I have exhibited regularly, both as an individual and as part of larger groups. I have demonstrated free-machine embroidery and exhibited at needlecraft shows throughout the country, including catwalk shows. I have had work accepted for Wearable Expressions, a biennial juried wearable art exhibition in California. My work has appeared in *Workbox* and *Stitch* magazines and I have written articles for *Workshop on the Web* since 2004. I am a founder member of Diverse Threads, a collective of ten York-based independent textile artists who exhibit together at venues in the north of England.

www.fibredance.com

27

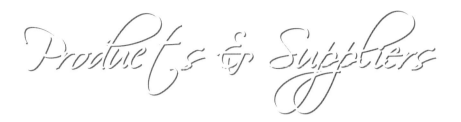

Funky Foam: craft foam readily available in colours and up to A3 in size, one thickness.

Plastazote: An acid-free thermoplastic foam, various sizes and thicknesses.

Softsculpt: thermoplastic foam available in single sheets, black or white, thick or thin.

Tyvek: A material of compressed polyethylene fibres and produced in various thicknesses and qualities.

Pelmet Vilene: A non-woven stiff material readily available.

Barnyarns - Madeira and Coats threads, Funky Foam.
www.barnyarns.com

Duttons for Buttons - Buttons and haberdashery.
www.duttonsforbuttons.co.uk

Kernowcraft - Semi-precious stones, jewellery findings, etc.
www.kernowcraft.com

Lords Sewing Centre, Oswaldtwistle Mills - Machine embroidery supplies.
www.lordsewing.co.uk

Painters of Liskeard - Softsculpt, art supplies.
www.craft-box.com

Pentonville Rubber - Plastazote.
www.pentonvillerubber.co.uk

Whaleys - Fabrics, dissolving film.
www.whaleys-bradford.ltd.uk

# Acknowledgements

Thanks to my husband, Dave, for his unfailing support and great tolerance for the mess I make and to Richard Evans for his full and freely given answers to my pestering questions on photographic equipment.

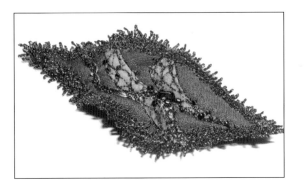

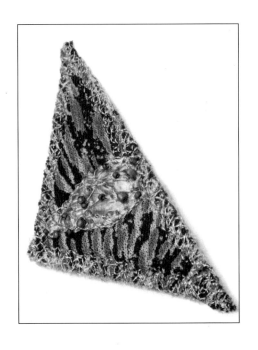